THE MAN WHO SLEPT THROUGH A SERMON

Acts 20:7-12   FOR CHILDREN

Written by Evelyn Marxhausen
Illustrated by Don Kueker

ARCH BOOKS
Copyright © 1979 Concordia Publishing House, St. Louis, Missouri
MANUFACTURED IN THE UNITED STATES OF AMERICA
ALL RIGHTS RESERVED
ISBN 0-570-06128-8

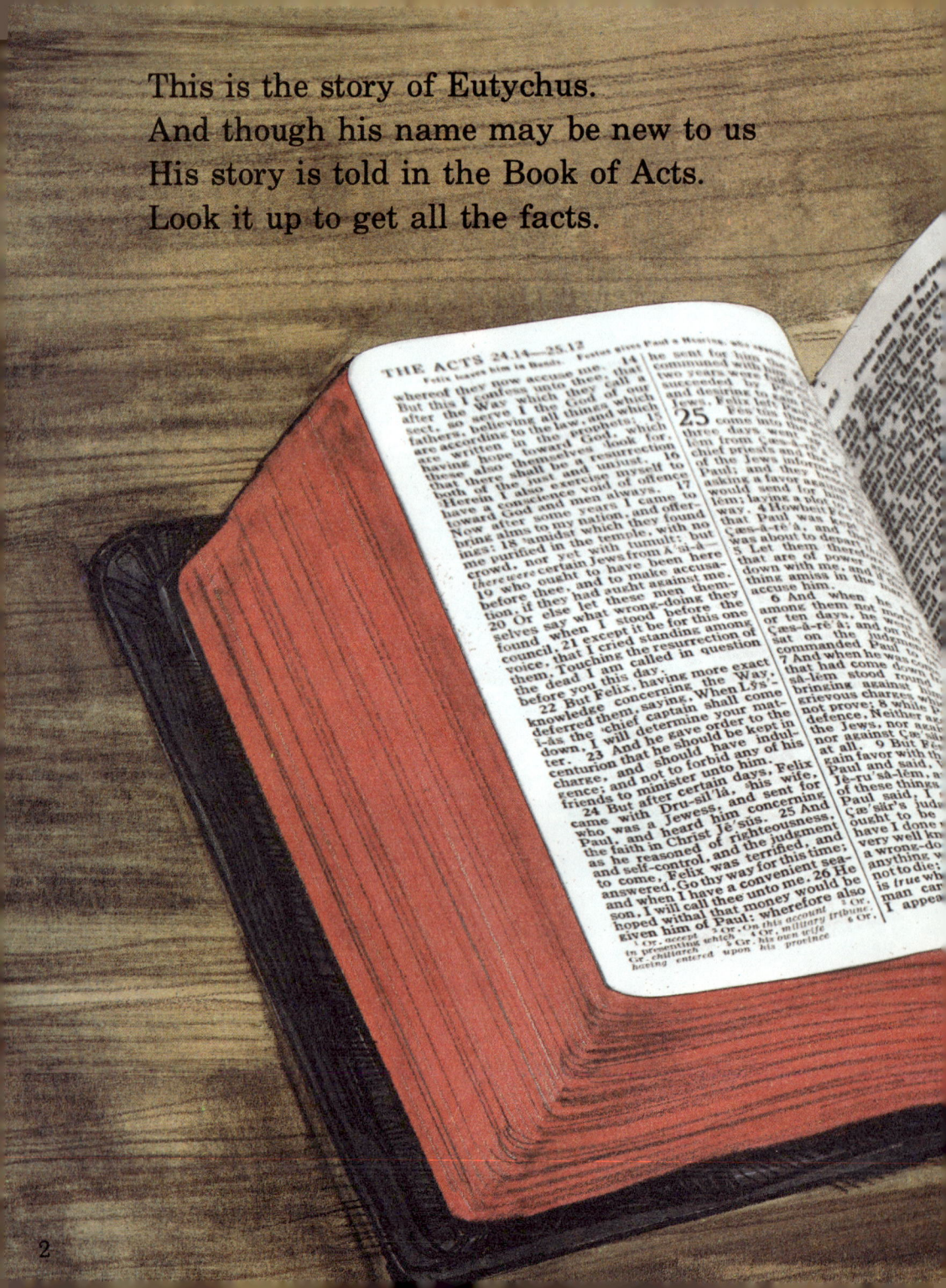

This is the story of Eutychus.
And though his name may be new to us
His story is told in the Book of Acts.
Look it up to get all the facts.

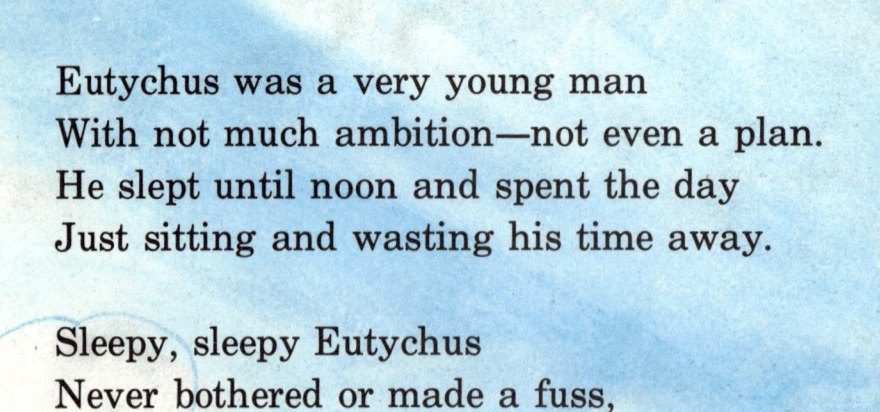

Eutychus was a very young man
With not much ambition—not even a plan.
He slept until noon and spent the day
Just sitting and wasting his time away.

Sleepy, sleepy Eutychus
Never bothered or made a fuss,
Just slept under the sycamore tree
Outside of Troas, a little city.

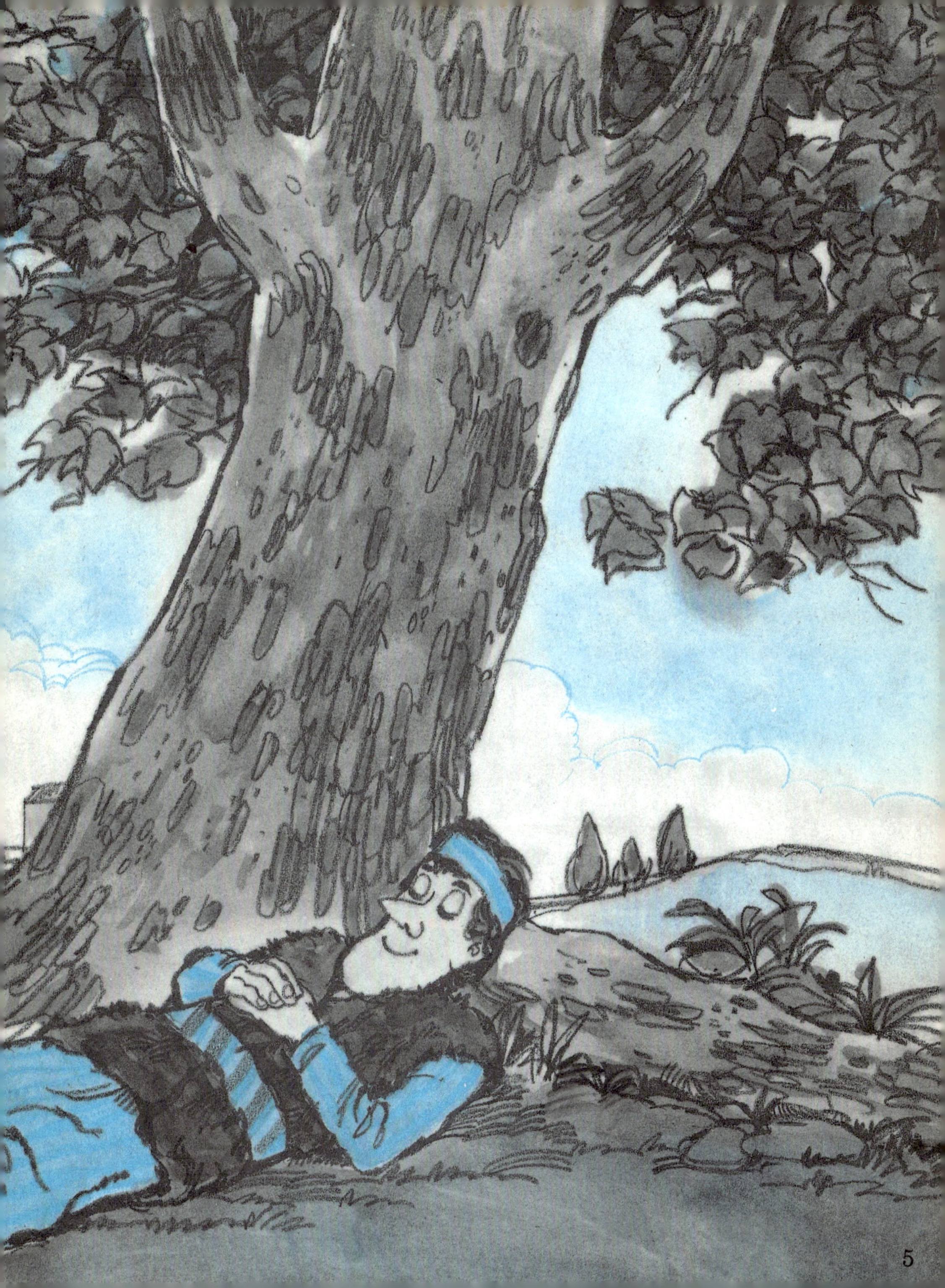

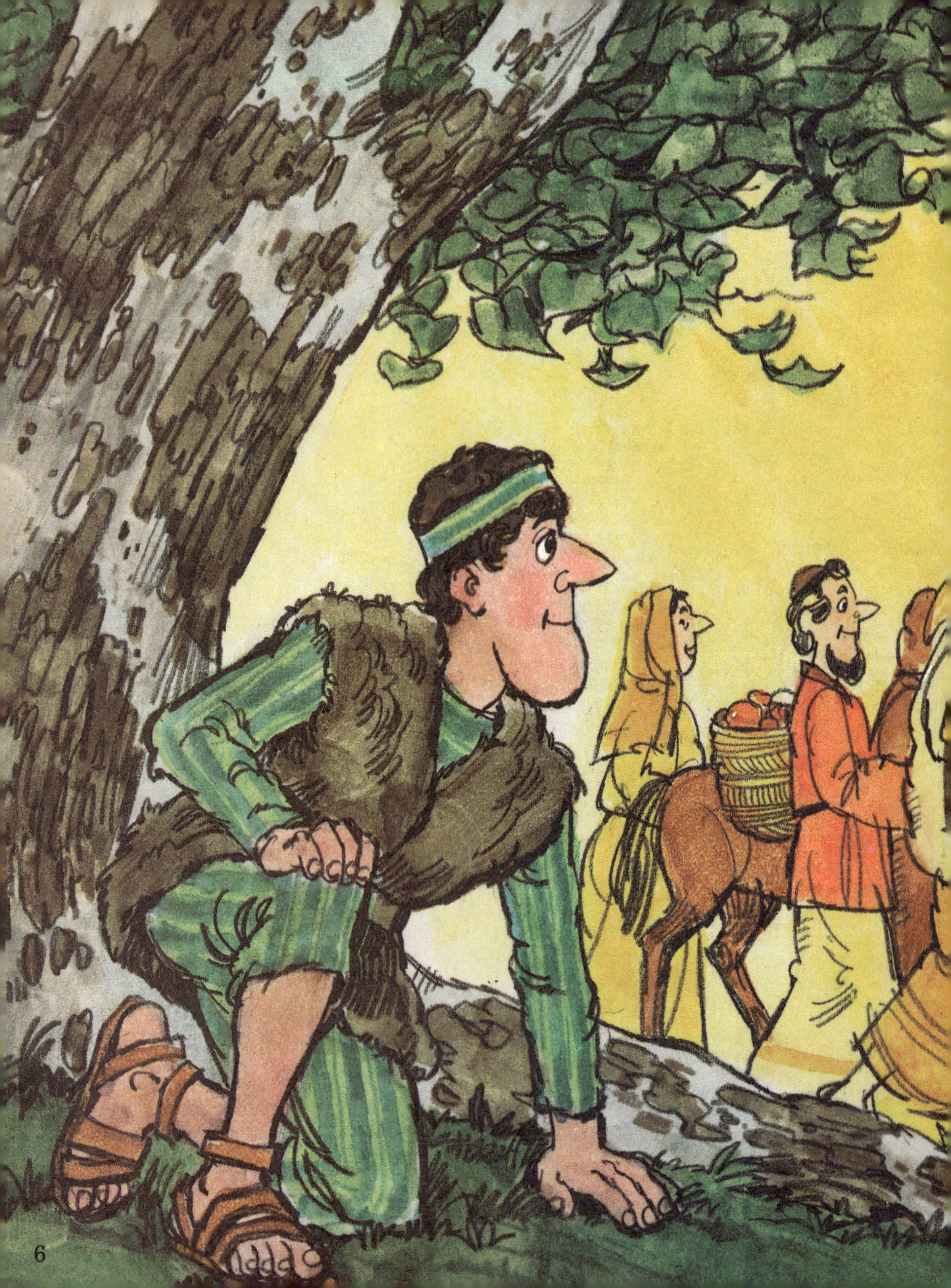

The market in Troas was busy one day.
"A man's coming to preach," he heard people say.
They seemed so excited, their voices were loud,
So Eutychus got up and followed the crowd.

"What's happening here?" asked Eutychus.
"Why all the people and why all the fuss?"
"There's a man in that building to your right,
And he's preaching there with all his might!"

9

He followed the crowd so he could see
The object of his curiosity.
He climbed three flights of stairs and there
He saw people everywhere.

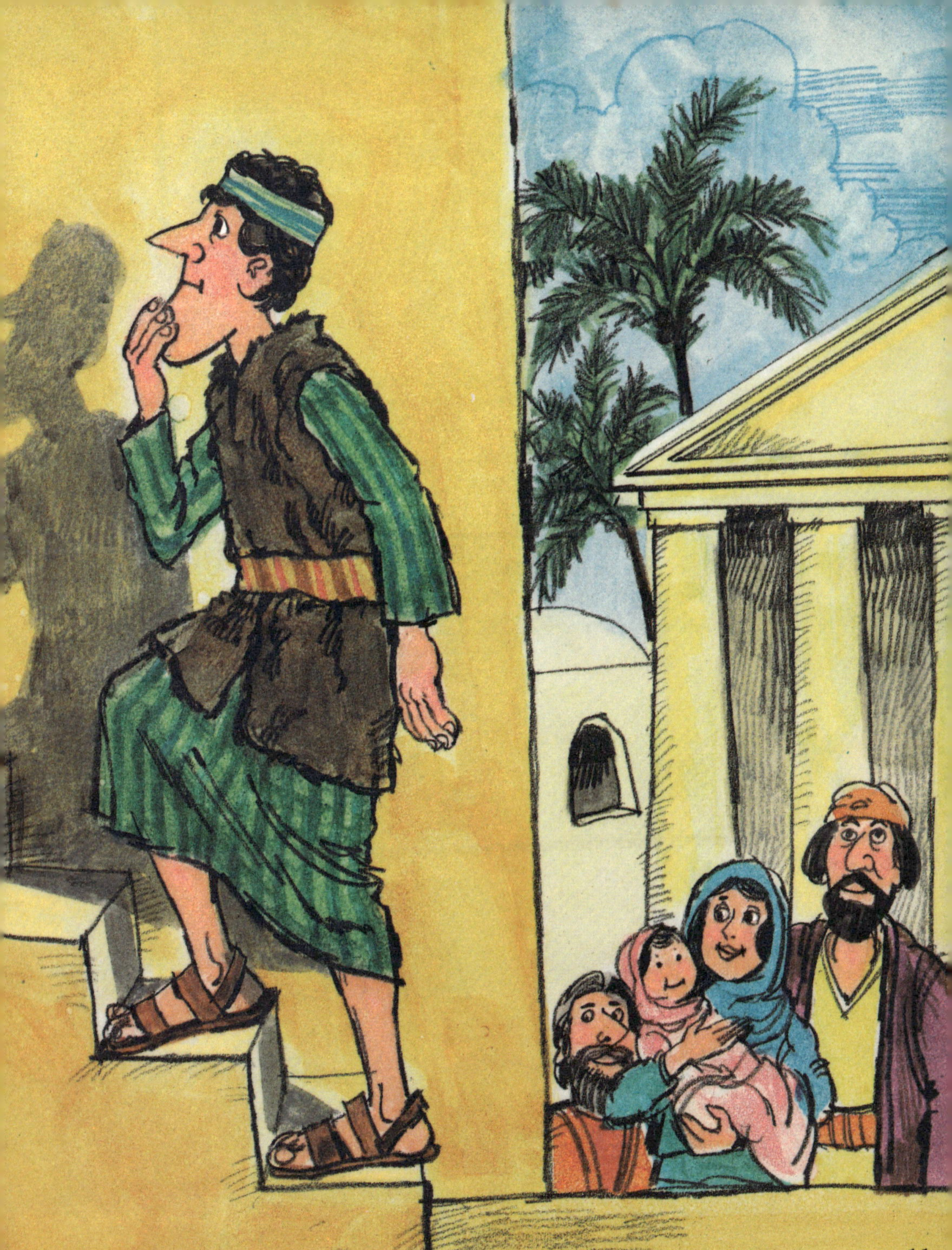

The place was so crowded—no room at all.
So he just leaned against the wall.
Then he heard a voice so loud and clear
Begin to speak so all could hear.

Eutychus listened carefully
But, oh, how he wished he could see!
He pushed and shoved and wiggled until
He found a place on the windowsill.

13

Now he could hear and now he could see
The man who was talking constantly.
He was telling them how Jesus, God's Son
Had come to earth to save everyone.

And now everyone could go to heaven
Because their sins had been forgiven.
"Does this mean me?" wondered Eutychus.
"Did Jesus save each one of us?"

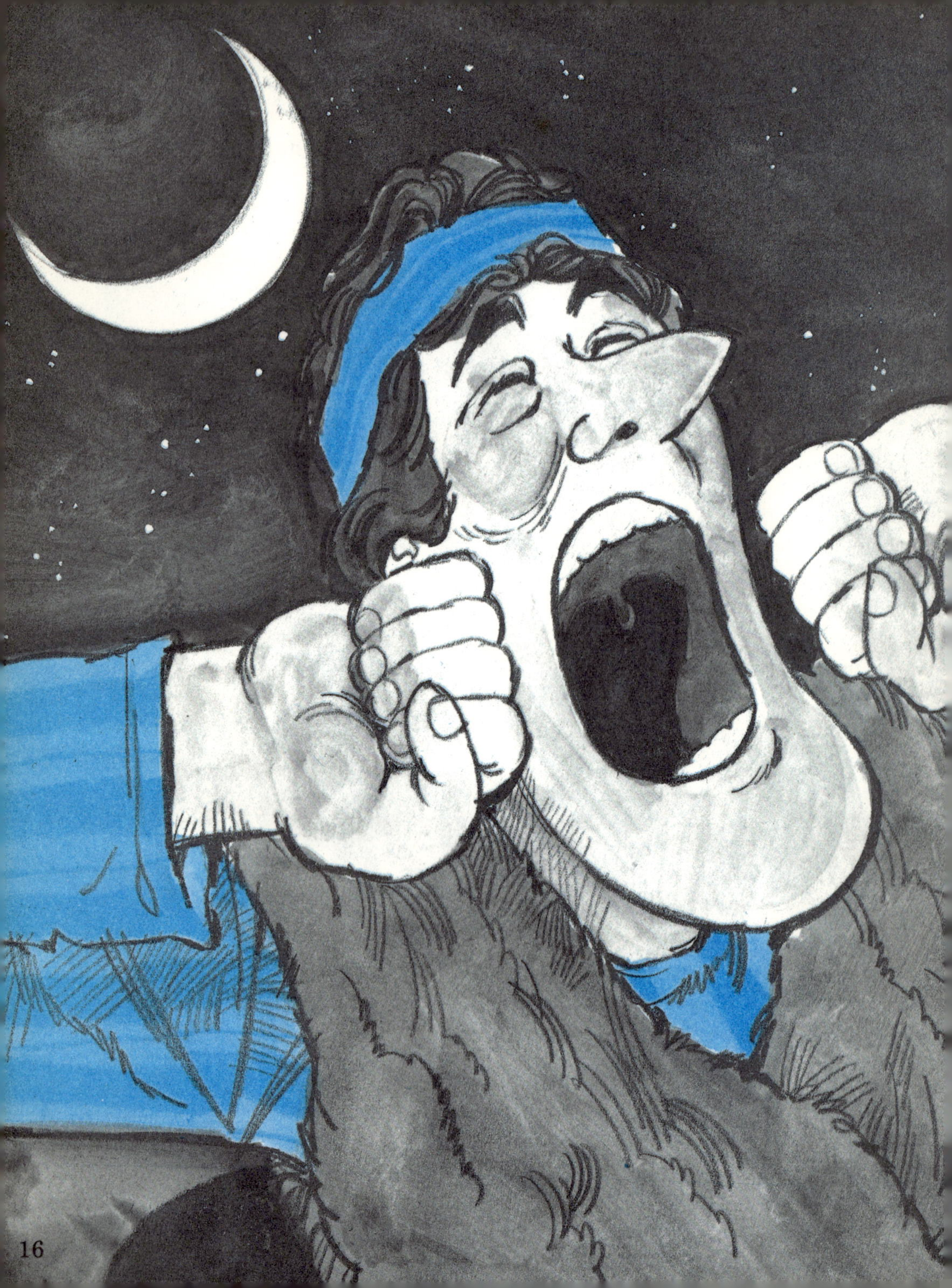

Who was this man who was preaching so?
He was the Apostle Paul—and he should know.
The sermon went on and on and on,
And Eutychus began to yawn.

And as he watched the flickering light
His eyes became sleepy—for it was midnight.
He tried to keep his eyes from closing
But the rest of him felt so much like dozing.

Sleepy, sleepy Eutychus
Never bothered or made a fuss.
And as he sat there on the windowsill
He fell asleep—against his will.

19

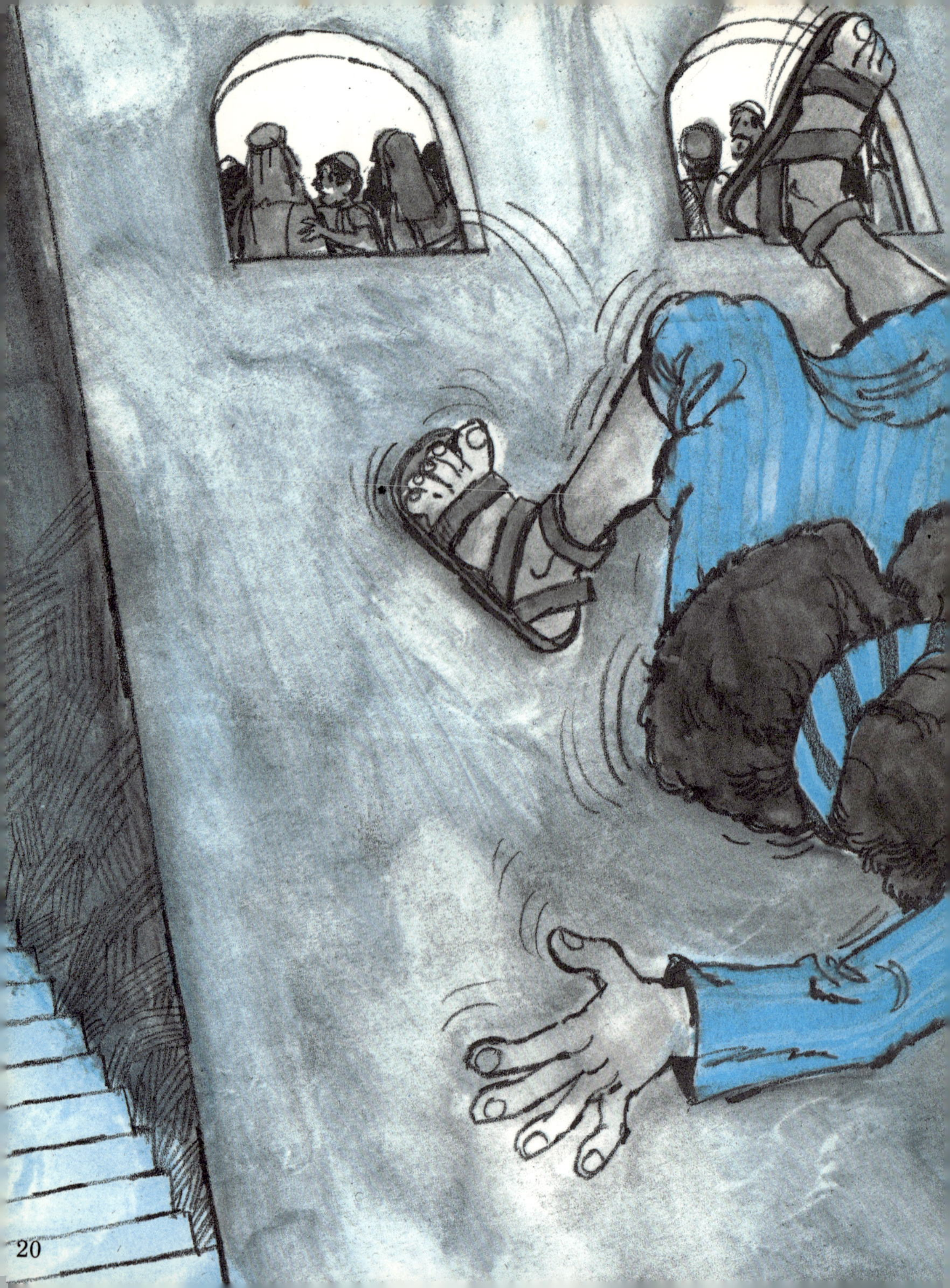

The window was open, and what do you know?
He fell three stories to the ground below.
The people shouted; the people cried
Because this poor young man had died.

"Poor Eutychus," the people said,
"He fell down there and now he's dead."
Now Paul stopped preaching and down he ran
To see what had happened to this man.

23

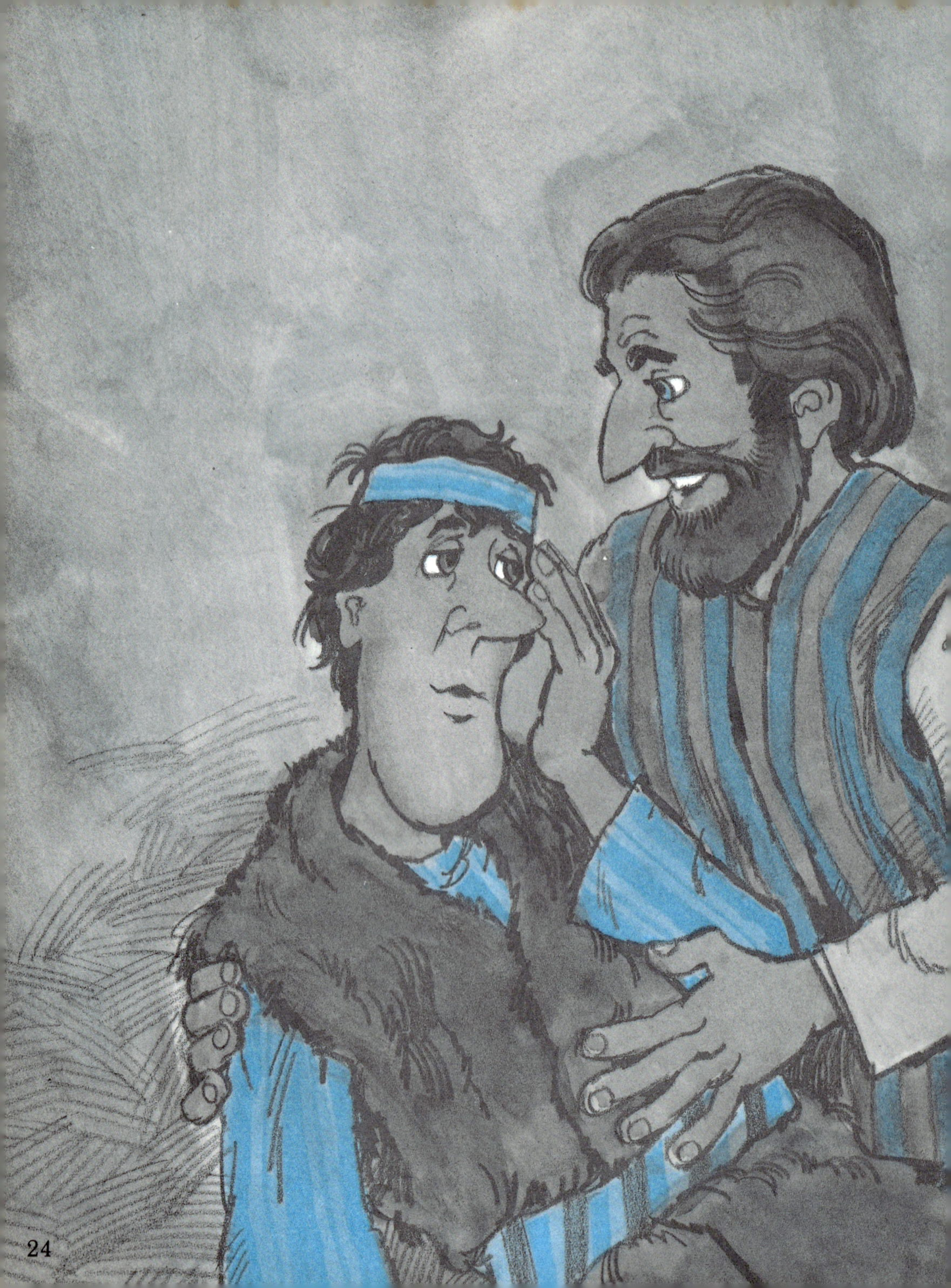

He gathered him up and hugged him tight.
He said: "Don't worry, he's all right."
The people stared in disbelief.
He was alive! What a relief!

Eutychus opened his eyes up wide.
What was he doing here outside?
He smiled and rose and said, "Thank you, Paul.
I feel just great—I don't hurt at all."

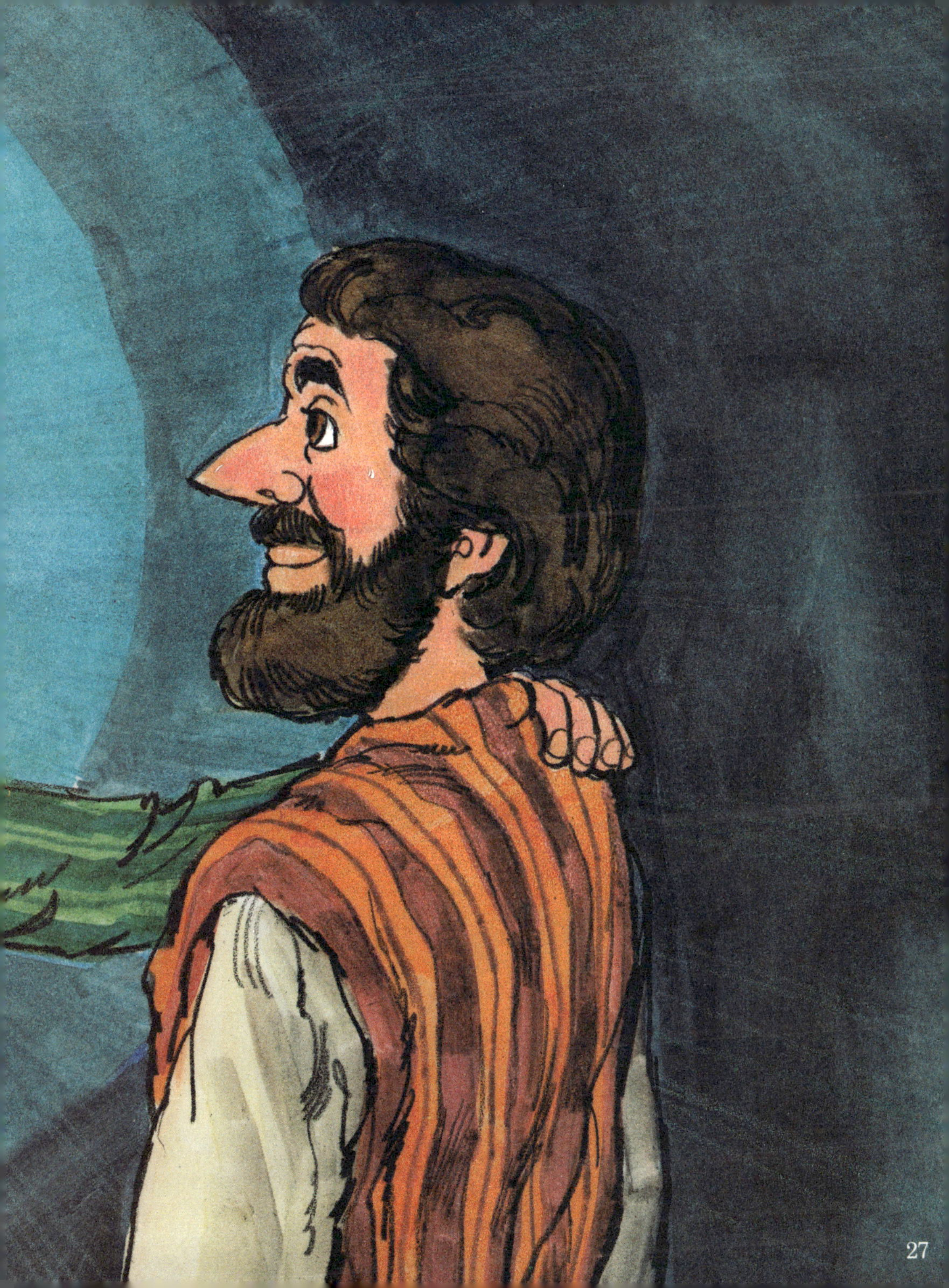

Now Eutychus was wide awake.
He knew he'd been saved, for Jesus' sake.
He wasn't sleepy, wasn't bored.
He had a job: to serve the Lord.

He wanted to tell everyone
That Jesus really was God's Son.
And how Paul, his friend, by God's own will,
Helped him when he fell off the sill.

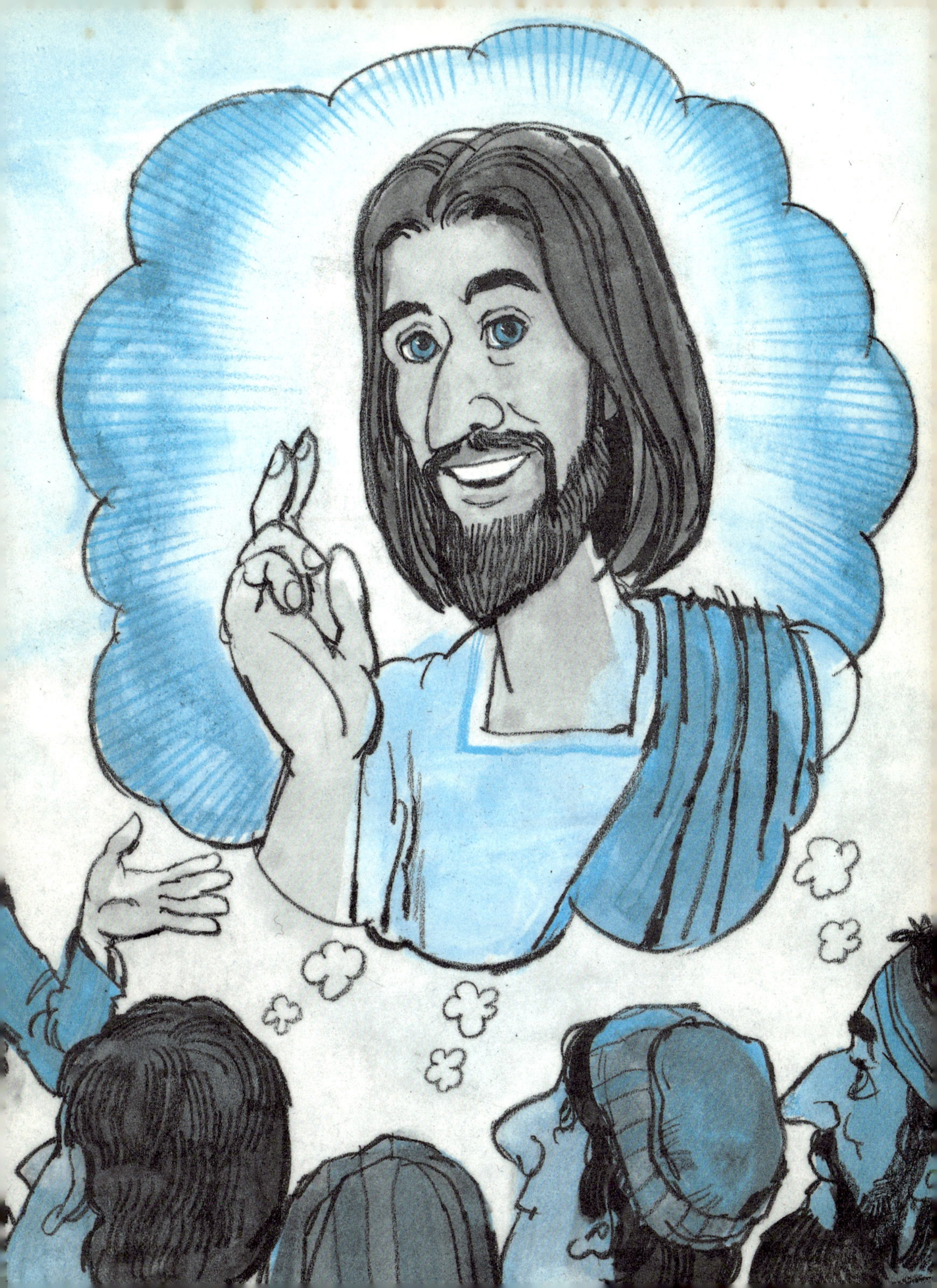

Happy, happy Eutychus,
Now he's too busy to make a fuss.
No time to sleep or sit in the sun.
He's telling the Good News to everyone.

31

DEAR PARENTS:

Paul had come from Philippi to Troas, where he spent seven days with the early Christians of the city. On his last night before leaving to continue southward Paul and this group of early Christians came together for instruction, services, and Holy Communion. It was Sunday, the first day of the week, and this is the first reliable account of Sunday being set aside as the day for worship. How fortunate this gathering was to have the Apostle Paul leading the services!

But apparently even Paul could not hold the attention of everyone, and Eutychus had the problem too many have while attending worship services or Bible class. Maybe it was the flickering lights, the crowded room, or the lateness of the hour, but for whatever the reason, Eutychus could not stay awake, and he fell not only asleep but down—as he fell out the window to the ground below.

We can imagine the reactions of the assembly as they became aware of the accident, and their fear as they rushed down to the body on the ground. But it was at that scene of the accident that they might have learned their greatest lesson of the evening, for they realized the power of God at work in Paul and the truth of God's Word.

THE EDITOR